Nicholle Carrière

Contents

Why Plant a Garden?

It's fun to grow your own food!

Vegetables come in all the colors of the rainbow:

- Red—tomatoes, radishes, beets
- Orange—carrots, pumpkins
- Yellow—corn, yellow tomatoes, squash
- Green—lettuce, peas, beans, spinach
- Blue and Purple—purple cabbage, purple carrots, purple potatoes, eggplant
- White—onions, potatoes

What Kind of Garden?

In a traditional garden, you plant seeds right into the ground. This kind of garden can be small or very large.

Raised beds are wooden boxes filled with dirt. You can put raised beds wherever you like and make them any size or shape.

You can grow plants in **pots** if you don't have very much space. You can put just one plant in a pot or plant a group of herbs or greens in a bigger pot.

How to Begin

Get an adult to help you measure your garden plot.

Ask an adult to help you write down how wide and how long the garden is. Then use the measurements on the seed packets to plan the rows.

Draw a picture of your garden using lines for the rows.

Write the name or draw a picture of the vegetable you want to plant in each row.

Gardening with Pots

You can grow plants in pots on a balcony or patio. You can use a few large pots or groups of smaller pots.

Tomatoes grow well in pots. So do peas, beans, radishes and other smaller plants. You can grow a whole salad in a bigger pot!

Remember that small pots dry out quickly. You need to water them every day.

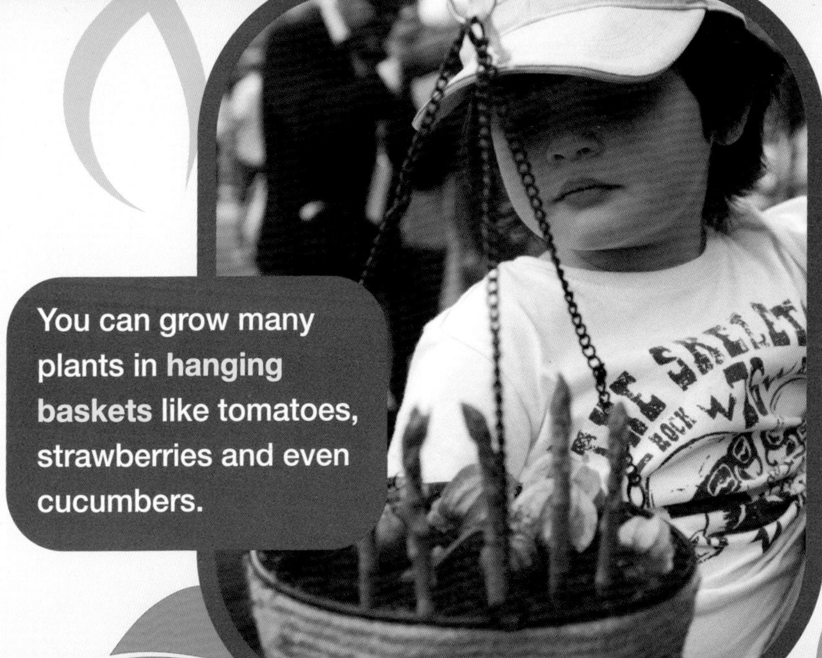

You can grow many plants in **hanging baskets** like tomatoes, strawberries and even cucumbers.

How Do Seeds Grow?

Seeds need four things to grow: water, air, sun and warmth. When a seed starts to grow, the roots grow first. They grow out of the seed and down into the soil.

Next, a little plant called a seedling pushes its way out of the soil. As it grows, it gets food from the soil.

The plant's leaves use sunlight, water and air to make food for the plant.

When the plant is big enough, it makes flowers. The flowers become vegetables and fruits like beans, peas, strawberries, zucchinis and cucumbers.

Vegetables like beets, carrots and potatoes grow from plant roots underground.

What do plants drink?

Root beer.

Pollinators

Flowers attract bees with their bright colors. Bees eat the sweet nectar that flowers make. They also use the nectar to make honey.

Pollen is a yellow powder inside flowers. It sticks to bees when they are collecting nectar.

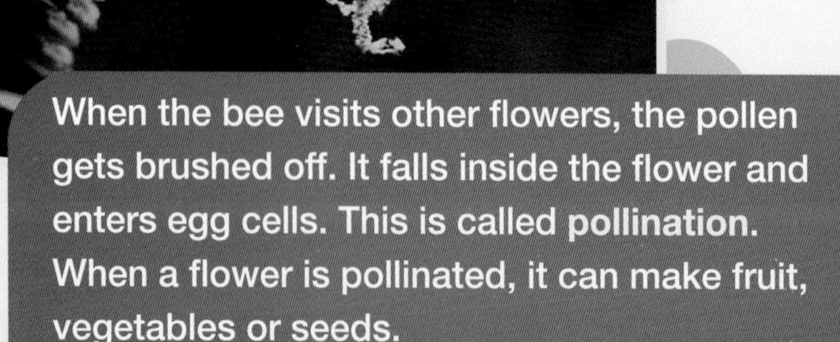

When the bee visits other flowers, the pollen gets brushed off. It falls inside the flower and enters egg cells. This is called **pollination**. When a flower is pollinated, it can make fruit, vegetables or seeds.

Other insects such as butterflies, flies, moths and wasps also pollinate flowers. So do bats, birds and the wind.

Without bees, butterflies and other creatures to pollinate flowers, we wouldn't have any vegetables or fruit to eat. Pollinators are important!

Gardening Tools

Here are some tools and other things you will need for gardening.

Shovel

Hoe

Fork

Rake

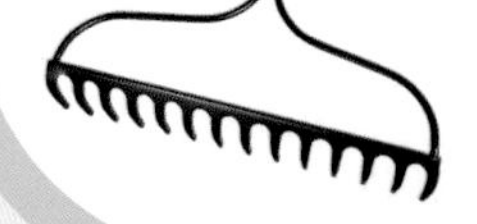

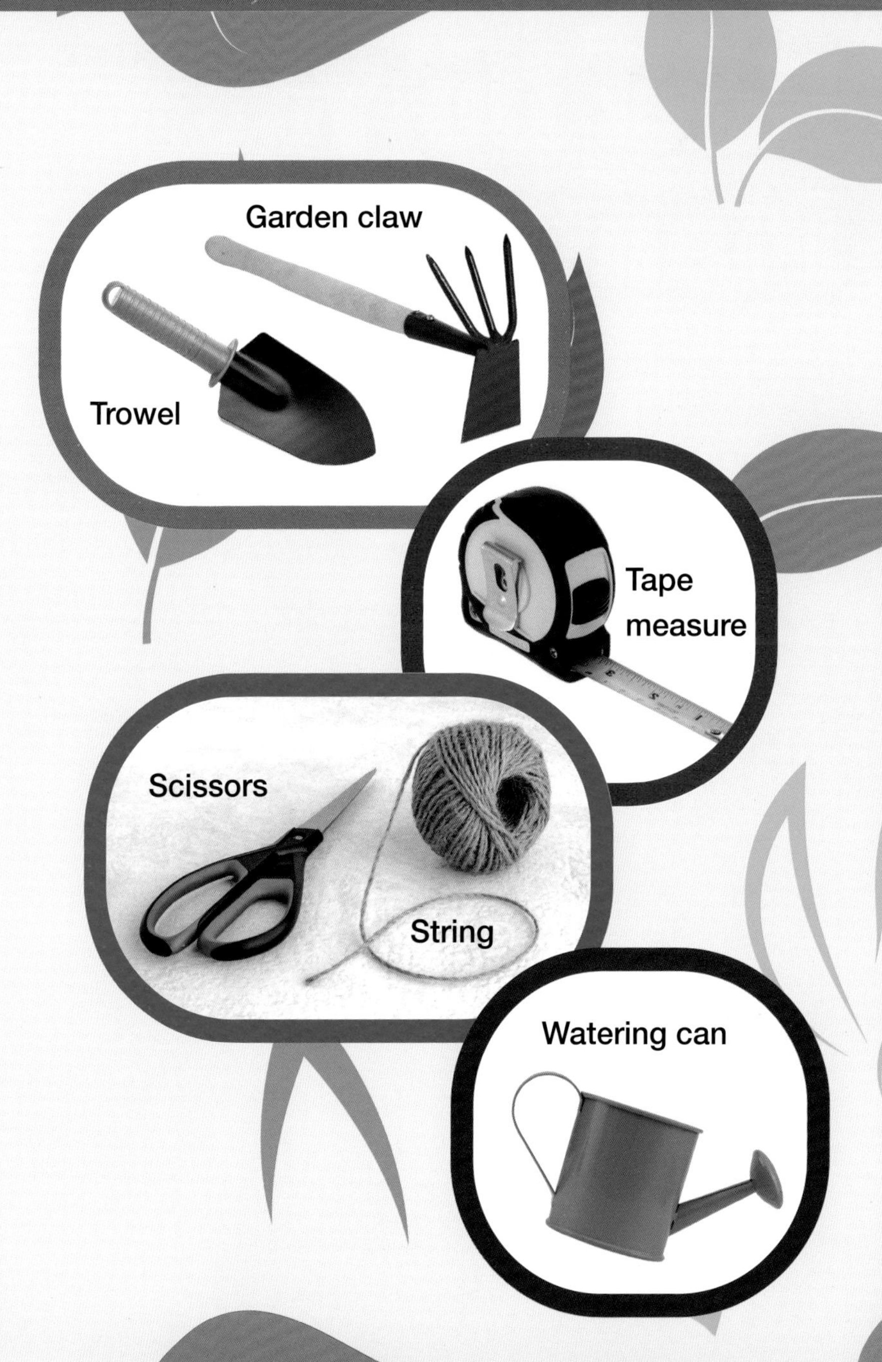
Garden claw
Trowel
Tape
measure
Scissors
String
Watering can

How Do You Plant Seeds?

How do you know how far apart to plant seeds? Or how deep? Or how far apart the rows should be?

Look at the back of the seed packets to find out how far apart and how deep to plant the seeds. It will also say how far apart the rows should be and how long the seeds take to come up—**germinate**.

To make straight rows, use two sticks joined with a piece of string. Put a stick into the ground on each side of the garden with the string stretched in between. Then it's easy to make a straight row between the sticks.

What kind of table can you eat?

A vegetable

Seed Packet Information

Everything you need to know about planting seeds is on the back of the seed packet.

How long the seeds take to sprout

How deep to plant the seeds

How far apart to plant the seeds

How far apart to put the plants (if you started them indoors)

How far apart the rows should be

A description of the plant

Days to Sprout	*Seed Depth*	*Seed Spacing*	*Plant Spacing*	*Row Spacing*
7-14	**1.3 cm (1/2")**	**2.5 cm (1")**	**15 cm (6")**	**30 cm (12")**
Jours à Germination	*Profondeur de semence*	*Distance des semences*	*Distance des plants*	*Espacement de rangée*

Chives form clumps of grass-like hollow leaves with a mild onion flavor. Develops attractive lavender-pink flowers. Delicious in soups, salads, cheese, egg dishes and with sour cream on baked potatoes. Can be grown indoors. Clumps may be divided and transplanted in spring after first season. Harvest often by cutting 5 cm (2") from the ground. Can be dried or frozen. Perennial. Zone 3

Fertilize with natural resources such as compost or manure. No herbicides, pesticides or man made fertilizers were used in the production of these seeds.

La ciboulette forme des touffes de feuilles en forme de graminée, creuses à saveur légère d'oignon. Ses jolies fleurs sont rose lavande. Délicieuse dans la soupe, la salade, avec les mets à base de fromage ou d'oeufs et aussi, bien sûr, sur les pommes de terre au four avec de la crème sure. Peut être planté à l'intérieur. On peut diviser et repiquer ses touffes au printemps a près une première saison de croissance. Récoltez souvent en coupant les feuilles à 5 cm (2") du sol. Peut être séchée ou congelée. Vivace. Zone 3

Fertilisez avec des ressources naturelles telles que le compost ou le fumier. Aucun herbicide, pesticide ou engrais artificiel ont été utilisés dans la production de ces semences.

Seed Packet for Chives

Watering Your Garden

Water your garden once or twice a week. Plants grow best when you water them regularly. Letting them dry out a bit helps the roots grow stronger.

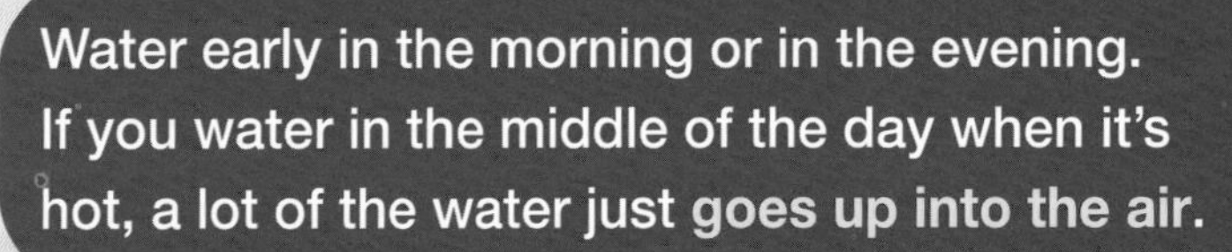

Water early in the morning or in the evening. If you water in the middle of the day when it's hot, a lot of the water just goes up into the air.

Plants drink water through their roots. Use enough water so it soaks down into the soil to reach the roots. Use a stick or trowel to dig down a bit to check.

Good Garden Bugs

When bees visit flowers for nectar to make honey, they also collect pollen. They pollinate the flowers, helping them make the vegetables we love to eat.

Butterflies also help pollinate flowers. And they're pretty to look at!

Earthworms make tunnels in the soil. This brings air to the plant roots. Earthworm poop is also good food for plants!

Bad Garden Bugs

Many bugs and other creatures eat the leaves and vegetables of your plants. The best way to get rid of these is to pick them off by hand. Yes, really!

Slug

Slugs look like snails without shells. They eat lettuce, spinach and other greens. They leave gooey slime trails as they move.

Aphids

Aphids are tiny green bugs. They suck the juice out of stems and leaves. They leave behind a sticky juice called **honeydew**. Aphids are a favorite food of ladybugs and lacewings. You can buy ladybugs at a garden center.

Cutworm

Cutworms are fat worms about 1 inch (2.5 cm) long. They live in the soil and mostly come out at night. Cutworms chew through the stems of plants. Sometimes they eat the whole plant!

What do you call a homeless snail?

A slug

Radishes

Radishes have a spicy flavor. They grow fast. The first plants appear 3 to 7 days after you plant the seeds. They are ready to eat in about 30 days.

You can eat the whole radish plant, not just the root. Be careful! The leaves are bitter!

Most radishes are round, but some are long and skinny. Besides the usual red color, radishes can be white, black, yellow and watermelon (green on the outside and red on the inside).

Beans

Beans are easy to plant because the seeds are so big. They grow quickly. You can pick them after about 45 days.

Bush beans grow to be about 1 foot (30 cm) tall. You can eat the long, green pods raw or cooked. Some bean plants have yellow or purple pods.

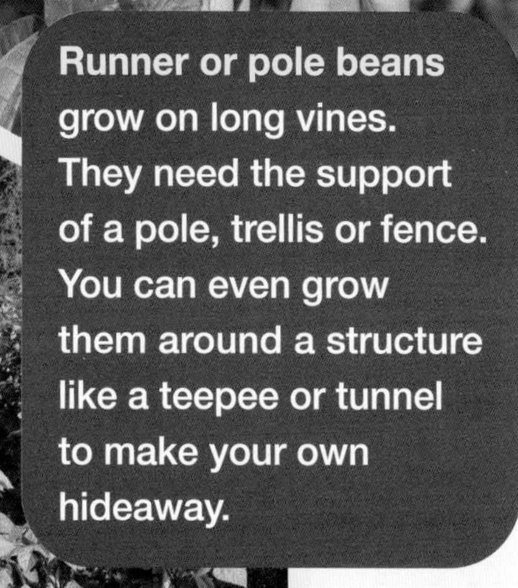

Runner or pole beans grow on long vines. They need the support of a pole, trellis or fence. You can even grow them around a structure like a teepee or tunnel to make your own hideaway.

What's the fastest vegetable?

A runner bean

Carrots

Pulling carrots out of the ground is fun. If you give them a quick wash, you can eat them right away. Carrots are usually orange, but they can also be red, yellow and even purple!

Carrot seeds are very small. It's easy to plant them too close together. When the leaves start to grow, you can **thin** them by pulling out the littlest carrots to make more room for the others.

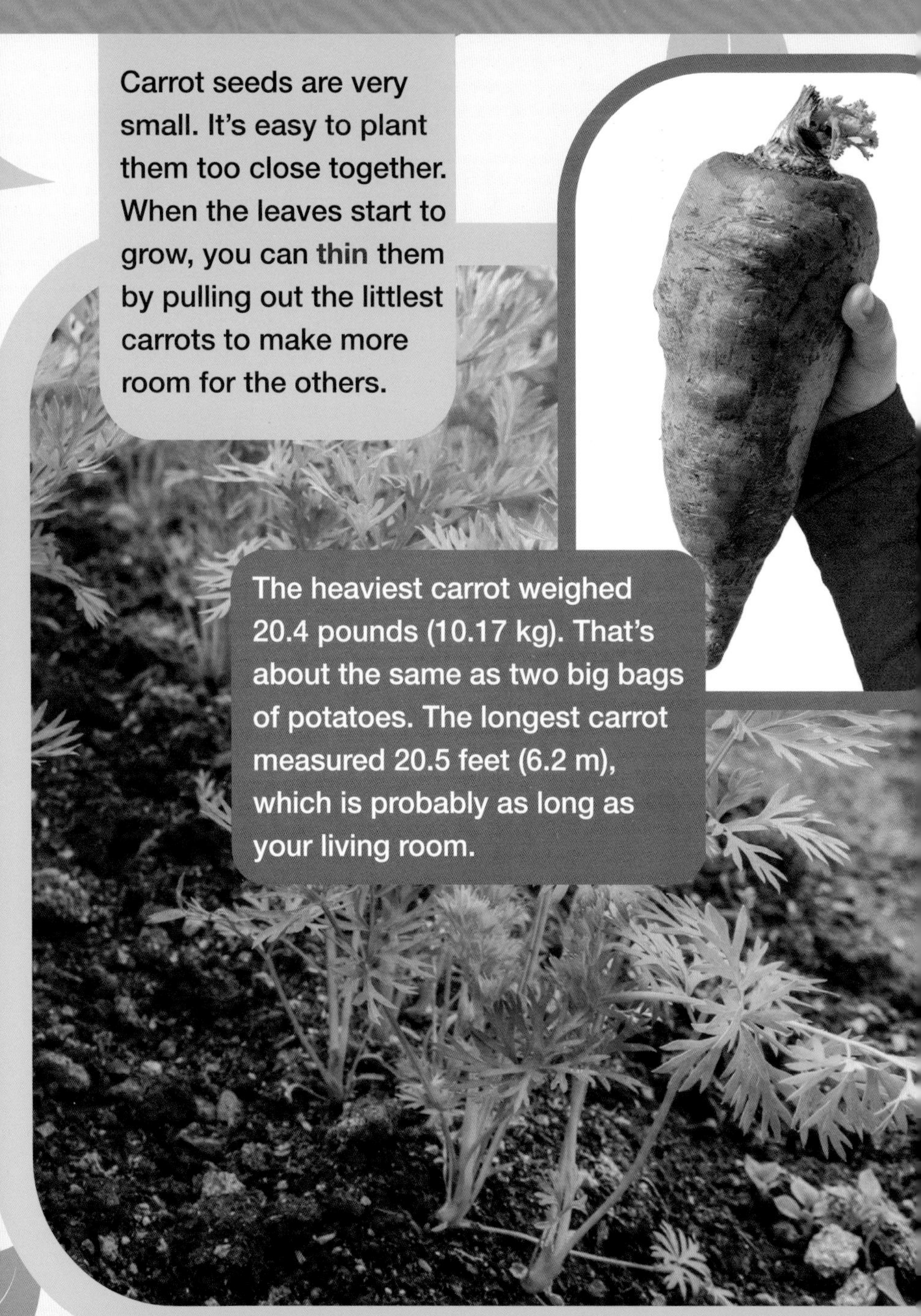

The heaviest carrot weighed 20.4 pounds (10.17 kg). That's about the same as two big bags of potatoes. The longest carrot measured 20.5 feet (6.2 m), which is probably as long as your living room.

Tomatoes

Tomatoes are popular garden plants. You can grow little cherry tomatoes, regular-sized tomatoes like the ones you see in the supermarket or giant beefsteak tomatoes.

Tomatoes can be red, yellow, purple or even striped!

Start tomato seeds indoors in trays or small pots 6 to 8 weeks before you want to plant them outside. When the soil warms up, plant the seedlings in a warm, sunny spot. You can also buy tomato plants at garden centers.

The heaviest tomato weighed 9.65 pounds (4.38 kg). That's about the same size as a cat or small dog.

What did the father tomato say to the baby tomato while on a family walk?

"Ketchup!"

Peas

There are two kinds of peas. Regular garden peas have tough outer pods that you open to get the round, tasty peas inside. Snow peas have flat pods, and you can eat the whole thing, pod and all!

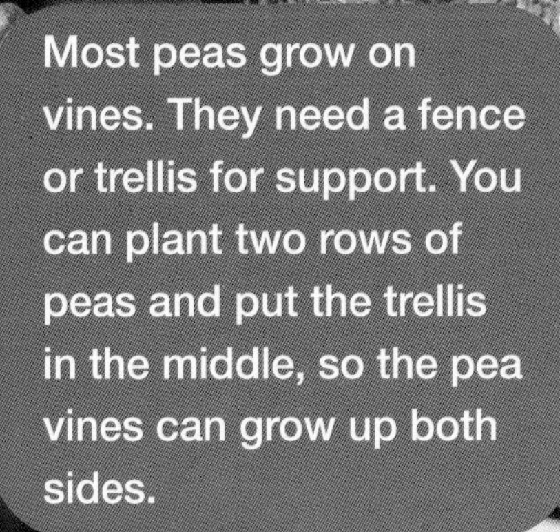

Most peas grow on vines. They need a fence or trellis for support. You can plant two rows of peas and put the trellis in the middle, so the pea vines can grow up both sides.

You can cook peas, but the best way to eat them is straight out of the garden!

What do you call an angry pea?

Grum-pea

Beets

Beets are a root vegetable, but you can eat the leaves, too! They taste a bit like spinach when cooked.

Beet seeds take about 14 days to begin growing. Once the leaves start to grow, you can pull out the littlest plants so the others have room to get bigger.

Beets are usually purplish-red. They can also be orange, yellow, white and striped.

Sometimes when you eat beets, your pee turns pink! Don't worry. It goes away in a day or two.

The heaviest beet weighed 53 pounds (24 kg), which is probably as heavy as the mattress on your bed.

Why did the people dance to the vegetable band?

Because it had a good beet.

Strawberries

Most garden plants are vegetables.
Strawberries are a kind of fruit.

Buy strawberry plants from a garden center. There are different kinds, but they all like to grow in warm, sunny places.

Strawberries grow runners. Runners are long stems that reach across the ground. Where the end touches the soil, a new plant grows!

You don't have to plant strawberries every year. They grow back in the spring.

Cucumbers

Start growing cucumber plants from seed indoors 2 to 4 weeks before you want to plant them outside. You can also buy cucumber plants from a garden center. Make sure you put them in a sunny spot. Cucumbers like it warm! They also like lots of water!

There are two kinds of cucumbers. **Slicing cucumbers** are long and smooth. **Pickling cucumbers** are short and kind of prickly.

If you are writing with a pen and make a mistake, you can use cucumber skin like an eraser!

What's the most uncomfortable vegetable?

Spin-ouch!

Greens

Everyone knows that leafy greens are good for you! They grow well in the shady parts of your garden.

Lettuce can be red, purple or green. Some kinds grow in heads, a tight group of leaves that you pick all at once. Other kinds can be picked by the leaf all through the growing season.

Spinach grows fast. Like lettuce, you can pick it by the leaf all season. Wait until the leaves are about 6 inches (15 cm) long before picking them.

Chard stems are like a rainbow. They can be bright yellow, pink, red, orange, purple, white and green. You can eat the leaves raw or cooked.

Kale usually has curly leaves, but dinosaur kale has long, bumpy leaves. National Kale Day is October 5!

What did the salad say to the dressing?

Lettuce be friends!

Pumpkins

You can grow your own Halloween **pumpkins**! Some kinds of pumpkins are small, but others grow to be really big. The biggest one weighed 2624.6 pounds (1190.5 kg). That's as heavy as a small car!

Pumpkins grow best in warm, sunny places. They have long vines, so they need lots of room.

Remember that pumpkins aren't just for Jack-o'-lanterns. You can toast and eat the seeds or make pumpkin pie from the pulp.

How do you fix a cracked pumpkin?

With a pumpkin patch

Herbs

Dill is used to make dill pickles and flavor other foods! It can grow 5 feet (1.5 meters) tall. The dill flavor comes from its feathery leaves.

Basil has a strong scent and flavor. The leaves are often used in Italian dishes like tomato sauce and pizza. Buy basil plants at a garden center and plant them in a hot, sunny spot.

Chives taste like onions, but you eat the leaves. They are tall narrow tubes with a pointy end. You can also eat the flowers. They taste like onions, too! Chives will grow back every spring.

Mint is easy to grow. You can grow peppermint and spearmint. You can also try orange, ginger and chocolate mint. It's fun to taste the different flavors.

What do you call a cheerleading herb?

An encourage mint!

Onions

An onion is really a kind of root called a bulb.

You grow big onions by planting little onion seedlings or sets (small bulbs) that you buy at a garden center. Plant the sets in a sunny spot. Space them 4 to 5 inches (10 to 12 cm) apart.

Onions can be white, yellow or purplish-red. The flavor varies from mild to strong. You can eat both the bulbs and the green tops.

Cutting onions releases something called allyl. It's what makes you cry.

What kind of jewelry do vegetables wear?

Onion rings

Sunflowers

Sunflowers are the tallest garden plants. The biggest sunflower ever grown was taller than a giraffe!

Sunflowers can be white, yellow or orange. The seeds grow in the middle part of the flower. Birds love to eat the seeds, and so do people!

Pick the sunflower heads when the heads droop, and the seeds start to fall out easily.

Watch Seeds Grow

MATERIALS

- Clear plastic cups
- Paper towels or potting soil
- Bean seeds
- Water

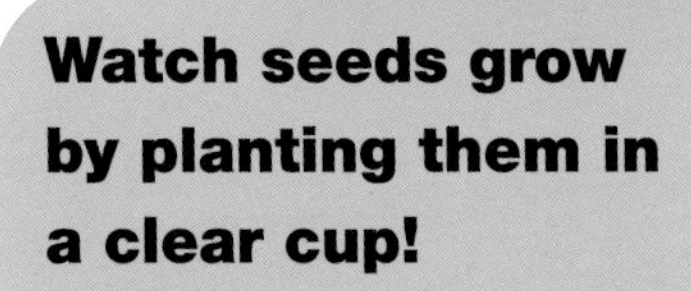

Watch seeds grow by planting them in a clear cup!

Crumple up some paper towels and put them in the cup. Add some water so the paper towels are wet all the way through.

If you're using potting soil, fill the cups but leave some space at the top. Then water the soil so it is moist.

Choose three or four bean seeds. Make sure they aren't split. Put them into the cup between the side of the cup and the paper towels or soil so you can see them.

Put the cup in a sunny spot and watch the seeds grow! After a few days, you'll see the roots sprout first, and then the stem will start growing.

Eggshell Garden

MATERIALS

- Eggshells
- Egg carton
- Potting soil
- Seeds

You can start plants indoors using eggshells and an egg carton.

Ask an adult to save up some eggshells for this activity. First crack the eggs in half and rinse out the shells.

Put the shells in the egg carton. Use a spoon to fill the shells with potting soil. Plant two or three seeds in each one.

Water the eggshells just enough so the soil is moist all the way through. Don't make them too wet.

Put the carton in a sunny place. The plants should start to grow in about a week. Be sure to keep the soil moist. Don't let it dry out!

Garden Row Markers

MATERIALS

Colored craft sticks

Felt markers

How do you remember which plants are in each row of your garden? Make some colorful row markers!

Decide which colors you want to use. You can use a different color for each vegetable.

Write the names of the vegetables on the sticks with a marker. Put the sticks at the ends of the garden rows and watch your plants grow!

Bug Hunt

MATERIALS

Magnifying glass

Paper and pencil

Camera or phone (optional)

Gardens are full of life! Be a detective and take a closer look at the creatures in yours!

Start by looking for flying bugs like butterflies, bees and dragonflies.

How many can you find? Watch how they fly.

Do they like to land on certain kinds of plants?

Take a closer look at the plants. Use your magnifying glass.

What can you see in the soil?

Are there any bugs on or under the leaves?

Are they eating the plants?

What time of day do you see the most bugs?

What's the biggest bug you saw?

What's the most interesting bug?

Do you have a favorite bug?

Funny Plant Heads

MATERIALS

- Old pair of pantyhose
- Potting soil
- Grass or chive seeds
- Pipe cleaners, googly eyes, little pompoms or other craft supplies
- Rubber bands
- Craft glue or glue gun
- Shallow dish

You can make heads with funny faces and grassy **hair**.

- Cut a tube about 6 to 8 inches (15 to 20 cm) long from the pantyhose.
- Tie a knot in one end.
- Turn the tube inside out. It will look like a little bag.

- Put a few teaspoons of seeds in the bag.
- Fill the rest of the bag with potting soil and tie the end closed.
- Shape it to look like a round head. You can twist parts of the bag to make ears and a nose.
- Use rubber bands to hold them in place.

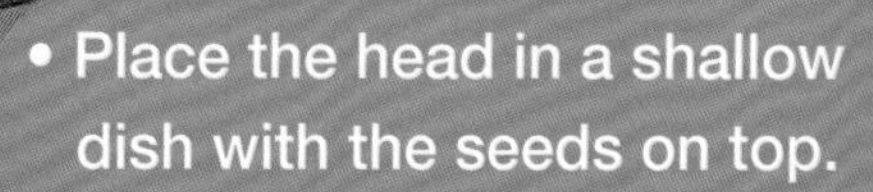

- Place the head in a shallow dish with the seeds on top.
- Use the craft supplies and glue to make a face.

- After the glue is dry, carefully water the head and put it in a warm, sunny place. The seeds should start to grow in a few days.
- Once the **hair** has grown, you can give it a haircut or hairstyle.

Printed in China

Distributed by: Canada Book Distributors - Booklogic
www.canadabookdistributors.com
www.lonepinepublishing.com
Tel: 1-800-661-9017

Library and Archives Canada Cataloguing in Publication
Title: My first garden : activities for children 3 to 6 years / Nicholle Carrière.
Names: Carrière, Nicholle, 1961- author.
Identifiers: Canadiana 20210301651 | ISBN 9781774510094 (softcover)
Subjects: LCSH: Gardening for children—Juvenile literature. | LCSH: Gardening—Juvenile literature. | LCSH: Gardens—Juvenile literature.
Classification: LCC SB457 .C37 2022 | DDC j635—dc23

Cover Images: Front cover: From GettyImages: Yana Tatevosian.
Back cover: From GettyImages: travnikovstudio, Zaikina, AwesomeShotz.
Backgrounds: From GettyImages: MrsWilkins
Cartoon vegetables: From GettyImages: Tetiana Lazunova; VikiVector; the8monkey; luplupme
Cartoon bugs: From GettyImages: worldofvector

Photo credits: Nicholle Carriere, 21. From GettyImages: Marco Antonio Gonzalez Lopez, 10; onfilm, 11; victorass88,8; bonchan, 29; Aleksandr_Kravtsov, 27; BlackSalmon, 23; Winai_Tepsuttinun, 54; 1550539, 17; Sushiman, 9; Liudmyla Liudmyla, 17;DEBOVE SOPHIE, 30; Svetlana Monyakova,49; in8finity, 55; Ibrix, 13; Niran_pr, 50; Veni vidi...shoot, 17; LightFieldStudios, 60; MNStudio, 4; Nigel Stripe, 17; Akchamczuk, 27; ETIENJones, 31; ETIENJones, 36; Yana Tatevosian, 38; Dinesh kumar, 15; Amy Mitchell, 44; Yurii Sliusar, 33; LindasPhotography, 45; Liudmila Chendekova, 35; romrodinka, 22; YakobchukOlena, 6; Vitaliy Krivchikov, 39; Elena Gurova, 34; Black_Kira, 58; showcake, 25; Evgeniya Evdokimova, 56; Akchamczuk, 43; JackF, 44; Natalya Stepina, 18; beekeepx, 19; Dirk Vegelahn, 51; Andrei310, 37; Halfpoint, 37; Zaikina, 42; Christophe Decaix, 12; joanna colvin, 15; Rudenko Taras, 53; nielubieklonu, 34; yaruta, 52; 140272114, 46; sgtphoto, 59; LightShaper, 14; BasieB, 31; typo-graphics, 48; AwesomeShotz, 57; Inzyx, 27; ndrewburgess, 16; SVPhilon, 5; La_vanda, 49; ChuckPlace, 39; romrodinka, 6; nilapictures, 26; Anatoliy Sadovskiy, 28; worklater1, 24; YuriyS, 50; Ocskaymark, 35; CandiceDawn, 30; taratata, 38; Ssvyat, 62; a8096b40_190, 14; bhofack2, 29; Linda Hall, 45; phanasitti, 16; etienne voss, 55; StGrafix, 33; drogatnev, 20; rand22, 47; AHPhotoswpg, 47; LeManna, 23; Sasiistock, 7; EstuaryPig, 25; Kryssia Campos, 40; Irina_Timokhina, 43; Ulza, 5; Diana Taliun, 41; threeart, 16; OlgaMiltsova, 48; EugeneTomeev, 63; hannatverdokhlib, 11; Olga Guchek, 51; bhofack2, 36; ohishiistk, 52; Alina Demidenko, 28; Jupiterimages, 5; Phillip Hendriks, 32.

We acknowledge the financial support of the Government of Canada.
Nous reconnaissons l'appui financier du gouvernement du Canada.

Funded by the Government of Canada
Financé par le gouvernement du Canada | Canada

PC: 38-1